STONE FRUIT

Rebecca Perry was born in 1986 in London. She graduated from Manchester's Centre for New Writing in 2008 and lives in London. She has published several pamphlets, including *little armoured* (Seren, 2012), which won the Poetry Wales Purple Moose Prize and was a Poetry Book Society Pamphlet Choice; *cleanliness of rooms and walls* (If a Leaf Falls Press, 2017); *insect & lilac* (2019), co-authored with Amy Key from a joint residency at Halsway Manor (the National Centre for Folk Arts); and *beaches* (Offord Road Press, 2019). Her first book-length collection, *Beauty/Beauty* (Bloodaxe Books, 2015), a Poetry Book Society Recommendation, won the Michael Murphy Memorial Prize 2017, and was also shortlisted for the T.S. Eliot Prize, the Fenton Aldeburgh First Collection Prize and the Seamus Heaney Centre for Poetry Prize for First Full Collection. Her second book-length collection, *Stone Fruit* (Bloodaxe Books, 2021), is a Poetry Book Society Recommendation.

REBECCA PERRY

Stone Fruit

BLOODAXE BOOKS

Copyright © Rebecca Perry 2021

ISBN: 978 1 78037 568 7

First published 2021 by
Bloodaxe Books Ltd,
Eastburn,
South Park,
Hexham,
Northumberland NE46 1BS

www.bloodaxebooks.com
For further information about Bloodaxe titles
please visit our website and join our mailing list
or write to the above address for a catalogue.

Supported using public funding by
**ARTS COUNCIL
ENGLAND**

Cover design: Neil Astley & Pamela Robertson-Pearce.

Digital reprint of the 2021 Bloodaxe Books edition.

ACKNOWLEDGEMENTS

With thanks to *Oxford Poetry, Pain, PN Review, Poetry London, Poetry Spotlight, Spells: 21st-Century Occult Poetry* (Ignota), *The Poetry Review, The Rialto* and *The Scores* where these poems, or earlier versions of them, were published. The first section of this book was published as a pamphlet, *beaches*, with Offord Road Books in 2019.

Thanks and love to Amy Key, Martha Sprackland, Rebecca Tamás and Jane Yeh for friendship, editorial support and insights. I am grateful always to my family and Ross for everything, and to my friends for being my friends.

CONTENTS

beaches (1)

you frown in your beautiful portrait,
appearing dead even at the time,
in a weak blue oval of enamel sky.
what's wrong, my little peach?
tonight a wolf's eyes will glow
violet in a forest you'll never see
in a place you can't know. is that it?
and, somewhere, is a whole beach
made of glass pebbles you will never
lie down on, nor will your skin reflect
its blue, green, white, and burn.

beaches (2)

the house is large and dark
with narrow rooms
i woke today unable to move my arms
and called for him

the house is a honeycomb
the truth is i feel robbed
of a sweetness laboured hard for

the house behaves
like a person hiding in a cupboard
with held breath
i hate for the inanimate
to get the better of me

today i walked the length of the beach
to the caves
and thought of him for some time
pathetic girl
how colourless a beach in the rain

my imagination my rage
quiet and unlike any other
said to him
you know a cave had another form
before the water came

beaches (3)

a sand timer holds enough sand
to last the duration of one human life
the oldest sand was already ancient
when the first amphibian crawled onto the beach
the term egg timer came to prominence
only with the need for cooked egg perfection
sand of three transformative minutes
a princess is trapped inside the sand timer
swallowing the contents
a beach filling her mouth
the princess likes her eggs scrambled
with chives and black pepper
she swallows the sand and thinks about that

traditionally hourglass sand wasn't sand
an hourglass is also a body
an hourglass body is specifically designed
for you to want to put your hands
around the smallest middle part
traditionally the material was
powdered marble and burnt eggshell
the princess fits in the sand timer so nicely
like a chick inside an egg
so much swallowing done
her stomach has become a beach
the yellow sphere in her centre
pouring through her smallest middle part

beaches (4)

the sky fell
in the manner of an avalanche
with all its occupants
my heart fell through my shoes
& dropped into the river
much to my surprise
my heart caused a wave
(navy blue basically black)
tall & elegant & curled
which my heart then surfed
the wave broke, the water swelled
covering everything in sight
covering my face
taking my voice with it
when evening came
following a very short day
my heart washed up
in the shallow waters
of the grey beach
much changed
among the detritus of aeroplane & satellite parts
it had an igneous look to it
smouldering at the centre
& smaller than before
a man, covering his dick with one hand
handed me my heart with the other
i refused it with a head shake
it smelled unfamiliar, sulphurous
it had been to places i hadn't
he looked down at it like an injured bird
humiliated

i began to cry
i found a large section of mirror
settled down in front of it
to have a companion in my sadness
only then did I see my chest
open & dark
as if a tooth had been pulled from it
i walked to the water
to wash
the water sealed up the hole
in my chest
the man waded in
he wore my heart around his neck
on a strip of leather
the heat at its centre was gone
but i knew it as mine
from its shape & hardness
& the way my gummy chest
called out to it
with a low humming noise
my chest a moonlit fridge
in a sleeping apartment
and a clock ticking
my heart suited him
the way it banged his chest
as he walked
his second heartbeat
he collected floating objects
took the time to consider me
as one of them
then moved on into deeper water
the muscles of his shoulders
seeming to hide furled wings
or compressed parachutes

a sudden feeling swept over me
who needed a heart
better to have the space for one
the power of that
i saw a dog
in the shallow water
its nose hovering above the surface
it came to me
making desperate noises
i said
sweetheart
this is a confusing place
the fur along its spine settled down
we sat together
who knows how long
eventually we felt like empty bags
like gone-off meat
things absolutely forgotten
down the back of the world
we thought of yellow beaches
of sleeping then moving
from the sleeping spot
& leaving a residual warmth
we thought of our new ghostliness
our liquid selves
without resources or luck
when the sky would reappear
how we would redraw our edges then
and with what

beaches (5)

people
orbit the griever
like a star
that might explode

elsewhere
the scuba instructor
once again
dreams of
last christmas morning

when he found a woman
face down
in the sea
felt it
bubble in her lungs
when he breathed
into her mouth

in his dream
the sky
is always domed
like a lid
and yellow

beaches (6)

this morning i saw a bee
out so late in the year
and all alone

a few paces on
brand new
early december roses

beaches (7)

having never lived by the sea
i have never intuited
anything carried
on its breeze: sirens, mist,
laughter
as the crabs boil

beaches (8)

there are things
you can say absolutely
a man should not be able to bear the weight
of a refuse truck on his chest

a clear wobble of heat lingers at the front grille
snow falls in the suburbs

there are matters of less certainty
will the crab come back out of the same hole
when the sea retreats
what similarity between crabs and lightning

when waiting for help to arrive
is it better to reverse a refuse truck
off the chest of a man
or no

a sand crab should not be able
to burrow its eggshell body
backwards through wet compacted sand

is it a man or a body
has there been a switch
is he pushing through
a very narrow corridor
in what direction

a sand crab fishes for food
with a feathery antenna
this is the manifestation of hope

the air is full of white speckles
the man's white trainers
are facing in unnatural directions
the truck is a dragon
the scooter's spinning wheel is romantic in a way

go home
eat half of a large meal
feel as if albumen surrounds you
try to wash it off
settle down to an artichoke of a dream
peel back its browning scales
the middle
i wonder
is it very soft

beaches (9)

my commitment to the city
is being tried in absentia
to the countryside
(with my favourite castle)
there can be no doubt
my commitment to him
hides in the sewer
with the rats big as babies

i observe myself in a new dress
marvel at its hugeness
incline my head like a virgin
organs a perfect nativity scene
all placed and vital and very still
feet not in frame

at the theatre
i smell myself on my fingers
the girls are really going for it
in their silver masks
a thousand eyes eat me
here's what i feel
that i, a mere stranger
to their new movements
i, a perfect stranger to
the curve of their wet backs
am a dirty grain of sand

in the evenings i am an orb
at the windows of my rooms
my ladies whisper in corridors

the lavender is uniformly wild
as it bows to the storm
the fountain flies sideways

you know how it goes
i love to fuck
my hands are my concern
i'll admit this much
in the correct light
and at a specific time
my head becomes the head
of a yet to be identified
woodland creature
most likely a muntjac
their eyes are green at night
and they bark like dogs

beaches (10)

this interminable christmas
                              most often i am alone at night
                              in my blue room
which is my preference
most recent rumour is a ghost came in the night   to fellate him
because even the dead like to please and leave a token of their visit
                              in this case
a black hair wrapped ten times around his penis
when the frost lifts a dirty smell comes off the river and in through the windows
ghosts have no blood
no flesh   no bones   no muscles   no skin as we know it
but hair which continues to grow and shed
i do understand that most people would desire not to be forgotten
increasingly i am drawn to violence   in the early evening
                              in my purple room
bad words in my books   blood in war scenes on tapestries
dead horses   impaled men and boys
people say   i am showing my ugly side
rumour is that the ghost was me because
witchcraft   soul already gone   ability to hear insects   impervious to poison
i think the exact moment of the death of love is not when its head is cut off
                          and lifted to the crowd
it is a cold stone in the stomachs of the living
ghosts have no blood but the insides of their mouths are warm with breath
at dinner the candles throw unholy shadows
a cooked peacock sits on the table folded back inside its feathers
the tail fanned and rigid
           through its numerous green eyes
i watch the room zing with warm-blood people   each avoiding my face
tomorrow we will eat another beast   a spoil of our small small war
the wall against my cheek is practically ice and the night sky is loveless

what am i trying to say
fear seems heavier in winter   in my hard room
as the swans separate   and the snow comes down

beaches (11)

on night shifts
my love fantasised about
throwing himself
down the central hole of a stairwell

never underestimate
the stronghold of abstraction
fantasies can have such visual resonance

the tessellated bookshelves
orange light
what a falling angel

but that was years ago

when i wanted a house for us
a perfectly square house
i wanted to paint the house green
like a plant
with the insinuation of a flower

beaches (12)

but now
phalluses of metal and glass spike up
through a city of gentle domes

(which are very few)
often housing marble cherubs
and pious women
and glorified men
which hold no interest for me
much as i might love the domes
much as i might love the confusion
in my heart
of a concave gilded ceiling

much as we two
basically exploded each other
on winter days
very dark winter days

my choir of one
didn't we reject
the uniformity of church pews
despite really never coming near them
despite never swallowing holy air
which it transpires is edible
like a long clean stick of celery

a room can twist on its axis
or appear to
the floor gritty
and the walls wet with a moisture

that saturates bricks
i said that actually
i wanted a house on stilts
in the desert
to sleep alone on a bed of cactuses
and to stop being a liar

beaches (13)

lemon juice
in your cuticle cuts
is not punishment
for anything
it is serendipity
it is one star crossing another
in a flat sky
essentially
it is god

lemon juice
lifts almost any dish
roll it on the worktop
be thankful
squeeze

speaking as a person
with almost no experience
pain can be
a gift

beaches (14)

if the city is a tight
and grubby flower
my friend is sitting
in the very centre
cutting her nails sharp
into ten translucent traps
waiting for the bee

The execution was conducted in the open air

I walked to the park after the blizzard.

The air had the muffled quality that follows snowfall.

No distinction could be made between the white slopes of the park and the bright grey sky.

The ducks in the pond tipped back and forth.

Their feet were orange orange. The water below the ice, a very dark navy.

The swans slapped along the shelf of ice that covered about half of the water.

Snow in the foreground of your vision takes on a bluish hue;

in the middle ground it takes on a hint of purple.

To paint the white of snow is only to capture the light that falls on it, as with all things.

. . .

The closest anyone has come to painting the colour white is Paul Delaroche in *The Execution of Lady Jane Grey* in which her dress is of such brilliance that the paint seems somehow alive.

The dress appears to glow very white, though it is, in fact, nearer to a yellow-white or cream. The painting, viewed in the flesh, is astonishingly large and imposing. In the middle of the dim room, Jane seems to hover, a bright, slipping moon.

The most powerful single point in this painting is the space between Jane's left forearm, which hovers above the block, and the palm of the man, Sir John Brydges, Lieutenant of the Tower, who guides her to it.

His thumb and fingertips touch her skin, but there is no contact with the palm. That small space, that rounded slice of shadow, is a pure and perfect manifestation of care and tenderness and of men who stand by and do not help.

The *true* most powerful point in the painting is the space between the mouth of the grieving lady in waiting, who we know only by her back, and the surface of the column she presumably wails at.

Wailing may be presumed because her arms are raised above her head and her legs seem to buckle. This point of space is a private one and therefore to be imagined and not described.

Lilac crest

My partner's grandmother slept for three days in the run up to her death, which occurred 44 minutes ago.

She didn't drink for seven days before that.

She didn't eat for three days before that.

Her eyes had been closed, most of the time, for around a month.

She rarely spoke, other than to the cat.

Although the cat was not hers, it was moved from a house near the sea to the care home inland, willingly forsaken by its owners.

The cat, fluffy and young and accustomed to roaming, moved from room to room on the first floor of its new home seeking company or attention or a portal to the outside world.

It jumped from the second-floor window and returned later that day, after many hours, unharmed.

. . .

In my dreams, I am often bitten by animals.
Usually cats and dogs, sometimes small feral creatures.
Inexplicably, I goad them.
They hang off my arms with their teeth locked in.
The feeling isn't pain.
It's a sort of pressure.
It escapes from my chest in a pleasing wave.

My friend, after giving birth, told me that 'pain' wasn't the right word to describe what she felt during labour.
But she had no other word.

. . .

When the house by the sea was being cleared of its objects, we dug up a Japanese maple and transported it back to London on the back seat of the car.

The digging took hours –

excavating the earth around the slim trunk, which was twisted like two ropes, encouraging each root to let go of the space it had made.

The tree was stubborn, though young.

Its papery red leaves juddered with fury or weeping as we drove home.

We planted it in the garden and checked it often.

. . .

The leaves curled and dropped in the space of a month.

We had traumatised the tree, which had subsequently forgotten itself.

It sat through winter – which was long and wet, with dramatic snow –

with tiny, outstretched bare hands.

. . .

For a while, every time I took a shower or bath, I was beset by a desire to bite down on the sponge as I used to bite down on wooden ice lolly sticks as a child.

Conversations with others have led me to understand that this compulsion isn't uncommon.

Many years ago a friend's cat, allowing itself to be cradled in my arms, suddenly sunk its claws into my chest, puncturing my left nipple.

I threw the cat.

. . .

We waited for spring to see what would happen to the tree.

The red shoots came and soon leaves, intricate and light, though smaller than the year before.

. . .

Her death was 102 days ago.

What happened was the cactus from her greenhouse flowered after 30 years.

The bird is on the garden fence and then it is not.

A crack appears in the skin of a peach.

An orange cat rests on the roof of the shed.

The fence is leaning backwards and covered in vines.

No rabbit

I once wrote a poem which appeared to mourn the death of a pet.

After reading it, a friend asked about the pet, which he presumed to be a dog.

I told him that the dog was a figment of my imagination, as was its death and the scenario in which I imagined its memorial:

the person I was with in the poem, the cold evening and the frost that formed on the grass.

The friend, a poet, seemed annoyed and disappointed.

He had wanted to be in on the trick

even if he couldn't be sure what would be pulled from the hat.

Lying comes with many responsibilities, or as many as we choose to acknowledge, perhaps none.

Or it needn't be called lying at all.

The two scenes I described in the poem were not re-tellings but I have, in other streams of time, known the deaths of animals and humans,

and dark nights and frost on the grass,

and being in the quiet company of another person in the aftermath of grief, as has practically everyone else.

The poem, in part, had been about how we manage death in ritual or through contact with the living, or how we fail to manage it at all.

The poem had also mentioned a person I love, though not in the context of my love for them.

I suppose this had been for my benefit alone: a private word with myself.

Perhaps that was the real travesty of the poem.

I have an absurd sense that love poems without pain in them are shameless, and that anecdotal honesty is as much a figment of the imagination as hallucinating rain through a dusty window.

Years after I wrote about the fictional dog, I sat on the shore of a beach very far from home, surrounded by small translucent crabs popping out of their holes

as that same person, the one I loved, walked with their back to me, through the waves, to swim in a rough sea.

In those moments, the sun was setting brilliant silver on the surface of the water.

I was thinking then that I was afraid of so much and them so little. Months passed and this was shown to be false.

More time went by. The friend died, the poet, and along with it his side of the story, the knots in the grain.

Memory continues to mix sediment into the water. Familiar smells disturb the air.

Light glows in from the hallway.

If you fail to close the door on a poem, how can it sleep? Anyone could look in.

Apples are ¼ air

My husband, the botanist, he dreams green. If you dropped an apple
into the ocean, imagine, it could wash up on an island with nocturnal trees.

The particular way branches branch resemble the pathways through
the heart. These are the things he says in the empty space before sleep.

How tedious to be a man; so perpetually unchallenged. He is making
his own kind of language only the plants comprehend. I paint flowers

in miniature. He tells me this is theft, a liberty and not only that –
preservation, which is contrary to nature. I find joy only in the shrinking.

Like a strawberry, he presents his pips on the outside. They are so numerous.
At night the shadows of his hands move like leaves on the walls.

He is a man made up of dark corridors, but he isn't a man at all. You can't
tell me a carnivorous plant doesn't have a brain, a brain and therefore a heart.

Perhaps now I am talking about myself. In his greenhouse he is so far away
like a man underwater, a man in a block of ice. When I dream, his mouth

becomes a pea-sized hole and I press the tip of my little finger to it.
I eat him whole. In the immaculate garden the sunflowers rotate with the sun.

On trampolining

I *Monograph of the cross*

When I was a trampolinist I never felt
like my movements
were really taken on by my body.
It was more like
my mind forced the movements into being,
rather than them just happening
in a way that felt instinctive
or magical or inevitable.
I still imagine that a really gifted athlete
becomes their movements,
as if the muscles absorb them –
no divisions or edges –
the brain an ice cube
melting into the body.

The brain is like a horse.
You love the horse.
The horse's nose is so soft
but it will throw you off into a shallow stream
and make you eat mud.
A gifted athlete is able to tame their brain
in such a way
that their thoughts become like water
by which I mean blood,
running into every corner,
but still under command.
My mind would throw me backwards
instead of forwards, trick me to land on my neck.
I was not a gifted athlete.

I knew it.

My heel failed first –
I was around ten,
seven years into my training.
A chiropractor treated my spine
by twisting my hip towards him
and pushing my shoulder towards the wall.
He treated my ankles and shoulders.
He didn't explain the relevance
of Achilles to my inflamed Achilles tendon
which I would later consider
a missed opportunity.
Why didn't he speak
over the crunch of my bones?
Perhaps he enjoyed playing the instrument
of the human form.

That little room of discomfort.
The high table with the paper cover.
The clock. The desk. The bone crack.

He asked to treat my neck:
problems pass from top to bottom.
I said no.
I had cricked my neck
the year before and couldn't walk for days.
My brother did the same and his lips turned blue.
At the next appointment my heel was worse.
The chiropractor said
he had warned me this would happen.

A few years later
a sharp pain shot up my lower back

when my feet hit the trampoline.
Once it arrived, it stayed.
Falling into pain is a strange feeling.
Jumping away from it,
knowing it is coming again very soon.
Choosing the pain,
being helpless to stop it.

I started wearing a back support.
It was beige, second-hand,
and wrapped around my torso
with parallel velcro strips.
It worked basically like a corset,
squeezing the pain.
Between routines a fellow trampolinist
or a coach would rewrap me.
Nearer the end of my career I was told,
minutes before I was due to perform a synchronised routine,
that I couldn't compete with such a visible injury.
The man who made this decision
and delivered the news
routinely marked me lower at competitions
than the other judges.
My mum had decided long ago that
he had something against me.
The support wouldn't fit under my leotard.
I unwrapped myself and
fell into the inevitable, open and searing.

When I was around six,
training on a Friday night,
an older girl landed on the trampoline
in the sitting position
with her legs slightly bent.

The impact smashed her face
into her knees like a coconut on a countertop.
When I went into the toilets
she was being held at one elbow
by my mum and at the other by my mum's friend,
my coach's wife, D.
The girl was facing the mirror –
her whole face red
with blood and her teeth bright white,
framed by the blood she was spitting out
and losing down her chin into the sink.
Her crying echoed in a flat way,
the toilets being in the basement
and windowless.
Her face was reflected
in the mirrors in front of her and on either side.
A multiplicity of red monsters.
Her eyes flicked to meet mine
in the mirror when I entered.
My mum told me, kindly, to leave.
The girl had her cheek reconstructed
with a metal plate.
What is the role of pain
in the process of learning?

About twenty years later,
as D was dying,
we sat around her bed
in a yellow hospital room.
Her younger son was my first
synchronised trampolining partner.
He was the only person
I never felt afraid of letting down in competitions,
sensing that we shared this missing part,

this part that was truly compelled to win.
He arrived in the room,
took her hand out
from underneath the neat white sheet
and held it as if she were still alive,
which she was.

A fundamental part
of successful trampolining
is landing on the central red cross
every time your feet hit the mesh,
which is called the bed.
In a single routine you land ten moves.
A move is whatever formal shape or rotation
you can achieve in the space between taking off
and landing again.
Colloquially, to trampoline is to 'bounce'.
Journeying away from the red cross,
the sweet spot where the bed is at its softest,
results to some lesser or greater degree
in an uneven landing.
An uneven landing means
a less stable return jump,
which means less height,
a more rushed routine,
a frantic spiral.

It is customary at competitions
for spectators to fall silent
when a competitor salutes the judges
and begins the first jumps of a routine.
The quiet is punctuated
by the springs creaking their extension
when contact is made with the bed,

and the tap of the rubber soles of trampolining shoes
connecting with the mesh.
A light tap. A very clean sound.

The perimeter of a trampoline
is covered with a hem of blue plastic.
This plastic covers the rim of large,
tight springs,
which allow the netting to give.
At one competition
which looked like all other competitions –
a large yellow hall
with very high ceilings
and brick walls painted white,
no windows –
a girl crashed on the blue.
One leg slipped under
the plastic and became stuck
between the springs
right up to the very top of her thigh.
I recall only
that her scream was brief and very loud
and rang out like a bell.

I am waiting
for the delayed collapse of my body.
A crumbling of joints and wearing of cartilage.
I think of it
like a shattered but still-standing window.
Trampolining, the GP believed,
is what caused my hymen to half break
then attempt to heal.
I went to him and told him
there was a lump in my cervix.

After he had checked it,
back in the consulting room,
I couldn't take my eyes off his hands.
As I was leaving the surgery, almost at his door,
he stopped me and said,
Vagina, not cervix.
I felt ashamed by this
correcting of my body,
that I couldn't even label myself,
my fingers on the door handle,
and carried my shame out into the world.
He had not been particularly gentle or kind.
I was in my early teens
and did not believe what he said,
instead expecting it to shrink
or grow huge and malignant.
I would check the progress
of the lump in the bath
then quickly withdraw my finger.
I hated to touch it.

And so, landing on the red cross
results in greater height in the return jump.
Greater height means more time in the air.
More time means
that moves can be completed calmly,
fluidly and safely,
with poise and style.
A clean routine.
More time also means
more complex moves can be introduced –
a double somersault instead of a single,
a double twist instead of single.
Marks are given for 'time of flight',

the amount of time a competitor spends in the air,
and deducted for
venturing outside of the red box
which surrounds the central cross.
I was afraid of the red cross.
I didn't hit it as often as I could have.

There are two VHS tapes
of me performing full routines.
In the first I am four years old.
My head is big for my body
and my hair is plaited.
I perform the classic Grade D beginner routine.
It is an almost perfect display
with a slightly whipped final move.
The video is taken at standing height
a few metres from the trampoline,
most likely by my coach.

After D was sedated,
we were told it would be
another couple of days until she died.
The older son,
a very gifted trampolinist,
fearless and elegant,
asked why we had to wait,
as if to extend the situation was a cruelty to everyone.
My heart leapt to him.
My coach, who had ceased to be my coach
ten years earlier,
said something to the effect of
nature has to take its course.
We crammed into the room
surrounding her and talked

about the life we had all shared together.
I wanted to paint her nails.

We went home, had dinner.
I stood opposite my brother
in our family kitchen
and said I didn't want to go back
to the hospital the next morning.
My brother said
it wasn't anything to be afraid of
and he meant it.
I couldn't imagine so sincerely
accepting death as a part of life.
I felt very ashamed of my
desire to run from the situation.
She died that night,
with her husband asleep in the chair beside her,
better it be done quickly
and with no one watching.

II *Prove balance*

Vending machines,
dim beige halls marked out for badminton,
strip lights,
carpeted stairs,
bottles of frozen orange squash,
blackcurrant squash,
blue crash mats,
motorways,
generic hotels,
rain on windows as jewels,
four to a room.

I once chased my brother
down some stairs into a hotel foyer.
He ran straight into the large sliding door,
which cracked all over,
then he fell backwards to the floor.
Or he bounced back from the glass
as if expelled by a spirit.
He spent so many hours
of his life
in these places because of me.

In the second VHS I am ten years old.
I am in the back right-hand corner
of a large sports stadium
at the World Age Group Games in Vancouver.
The video must have been taken
by one of my parents
or my brother, with his predilection for gadgets.
My coach is down on the stadium floor
with me, by the side of the trampoline.
By that age I would have been
strong enough to raise myself onto
the trampoline without assistance,
using the metal bars underneath the blue rim
as a foothold, but it's possible that,
given the magnitude of the occasion,
my coach would have lifted me up
and placed me on the edge.
D would have been next to
my parents and brother,
watching her sons and me,
down on the stadium floor.
The work of the entire previous season
had brought us to this point:

individual scores from each competition
recorded and averaged out to reveal the top four competitors
in the country in each age group.
I complete the first eight moves
of the routine and then,
dangerously close to the crash mat,
improvise two moves which propel me
back towards the cross.
It was a move smart enough
that I didn't score for an incomplete routine
or have marks deducted for hitting the mat.
To do those things
would have been utter disaster.
But it wasn't the routine I had registered.
You pledge a performance
and you must deliver it.

I landed in the vast
safe space between total failure
and absolute perfection.
I am an expert at dropping the reins
at the last minute.

We had travelled all that way
for those ten moves.
I knew the trip had been too expensive
though I didn't know in reality then
what that meant.
I land the final move
and instantly burst into tears.
On the video my arms
are held straight out in front of me
for two or three seconds
to prove balance,

and I am crying as I salute the judges.
I placed eleventh in the world.

It occurs to me now
that amid the fear
there must have been so much
joy in it too.

My white trampolining shoes
are in a box under my bed
with other things
I can hardly bear to look at
but can't throw away.
Markers of a different life
and time –
how quickly it is passing.
I have a birthday card from D
from about a month before she died.
She handed it to me
from her wheelchair
on a tram platform in Croydon.
She fell asleep after dinner
eating her cake.
Her older son laughed quietly and gently roused her.
Her spine had been reconstructed
with metal rods.
I saw the scan.
The white poles
set up like scaffolding.
At a house party
when I was around twenty-five
a friend knocked over and smashed
a vase she had given me
when I moved out of my family home.

When everyone left,
I stood at the door crying in the middle of the night,
as my boyfriend tried to retrieve
the shards from the bin.
It was hopeless.
So many pieces unaccounted for
or swept away.

We spent three weeks in Canada.
Two of them travelling Banff and Toronto,
making the trip worthwhile,
and the final one
confined to a sports stadium.
My family stayed in a hotel
and I spent my time with the squad
in a large dormitory, bunk beds
tessellated in a large, oddly shaped room.
I don't remember
how my family spent their time
while I trained.
In Banff I remember I felt happy.
I stood on a large glacier
wearing denim cut-offs and a sweatshirt.
It wasn't even slippery.
It glittered.

III *The Bad Gynaecologist*

After the incident
with The Bad Gynaecologist,
which occurred in my early twenties,
I became very protective of my body,
specifically the space

between my navel and the top of my pubic hair.
Protective like I wanted to shield it
with my hands
or separate it from my body
and wrap it in soft cloth
like an injured animal.

During the first part
of the inspection
with The Bad Gynaecologist,
as a feeling of uneasiness
began to creep over me,
I tried to distract myself
by looking at the fuzzy black and white footage
of my uterus
on the small screen to my right.
Looking inside yourself
and willing your brain to make sense of it
is asking too much.
The mysterious and private dark –
something you have only ever sensed –
suddenly framed in front of you.

If an astronaut had one word for the feeling
of observing the whole of the earth from space,
as did a human viewing their insides on a screen,
I think that word would be: no.

I didn't know
until years after my retirement,
at the age of fifteen,
that trampolines were initially conceived
as a means of preparing astronauts
for the bodily experiences

of being in space.
Training for acceleration and spinning
and the art of control
when there is nothing to hold on to.
In trampolining it takes time,
when you've learnt a new move,
for your brain, eyes, ears, limbs
to understand what is happening
to your body and accept it.
After years of performing
tens of somersaults in a row
you can land, pause, walk to the edge of the bed
and dismount
without so much as a wobble.
Your body calibrates as it goes along,
carries on as if nothing has happened
or as if you simply took a step.
But when you learn something new,
your body knows this is new territory.
Your eyes lag by a second or two
and your balance fails.

The Bad Gynaecologist looked
intently at his computer screen
as my body began the process
of losing consciousness.
I was now dressed and sitting
back beside his desk
wearing a complimentary sanitary towel
in anticipation of the bleeding
I presumed would come,
pain of that kind not seeming possible
without the logical accompaniment
of blood.

There was a time
when the existence of periods
was used as an argument
to stop astronauts
who experienced menstrual bleeding
from going into space.
It was known
that being in space can cause
muscle atrophy and deterioration of the skeleton,
slowing of cardiovascular system functions,
decreased production of red blood cells,
and balance and eyesight disorders.
Why not then the flowing of blood
back into the body?
Or the floating of blood
out into the atmosphere, uncontained?

The window above
The Bad Gynaecologist's desk was rectangular.
Very wide but short, like an arrow slit on its side.
Except not at all,
or no more than his pen was a sword
and the silver door handle an arrow.
All morphing into a collection of objects
for inflicting injury,
into a narrative of violence.
I hated him.

The Bad Gynaecologist clicked the mouse,
tapped a key – the room was turning white –
as he pretended I didn't exist.

IV *Blue tent*

Sitting on a bench in the walled garden
attached to All Hallows church,
my reading was interrupted by my benchfellow saying,
'I'm sorry but you have a...'
and pointing to the exposed skin of my ankle,
upon which rested a dragonfly,
gleaming in the early spring sun.

We both observed the creature
– which was really incredibly beautiful –
for a few seconds, and he returned to the lunch he was eating
from a tupperware with a fork.

Needless to say
I hadn't felt the dragonfly land on my ankle and,
even then, I could feel nothing, though I willed myself to.
The dragonfly stayed very still, seeming dead,
and didn't fly away even when, after many minutes,
I crossed my ankle on the opposite knee and blew on it gently.

I stayed on the bench
for longer than I had intended,
allowing it to be where it wanted,
wondering if I should interpret it as a sign.

I knew very little about dragonflies.
I discovered that they spend most of their lives
as nymphs on the water, and a matter of weeks or days on the wing.
In its bodily metamorphosis,
a dragonfly carries its nymph brain into its new form.
When I close my eyes
I can also inhabit my younger body with ease;

I remember the feeling of my nose touching my knees
when I stretched before training.
I recall the weight of a gymnastics coach,
hard hands on my back pushing me down into splits.
I have physical recollection of every move I ever knew how to do.

In the months following the incident with the dragonfly,
I sensed it was becoming bluer with each remembering.
I developed a wish to have touched it with a finger
and question what it wanted,
though I'd had no such compulsion at the time.
It had been stubborn,
like a grief that wouldn't break.
Perhaps it was simply presenting itself.

V *Glossary of competitive anxiety terms*

State anxiety
As small children, having stayed
at my grandparents' flat for the night,
my brother and I woke to discover
that an infection had glued his eyes shut during the night.
The skin of his eyelids stretched
with the effort to open them,
my baby mole brother, trying to come into the light.
He was very calm. I soaked some tissue in milk
and dabbed it on his eyes.
Slowly, small gaps appeared beneath his eyelashes
as the two lids became unstuck.

Trait anxiety
I was afraid of one of my coaches.
When I was told she wasn't due at a session

I didn't believe it
and looked at the door of the sports hall
constantly throughout the session,
waiting for her to manifest
like a ghost at the strike of midnight.

Cognitive anxiety
Me and my brother
were very different children who both,
in phases, had small facial tics
that our parents gently tried to police out of existence.

Threat
As a child, I had a large, yellow book of stories
which, for a while, I read nightly.
One story, whose exact beginning escapes me,
ended with a beast and a young girl
walking for miles through the wilderness.
The beast, to make the way safe for them,
goes ahead to vanquish an enemy in a duel.
The young girl is instructed to wait for him
on a fallen tree trunk.
She is not to move in any way,
not even to blink,
until he returns to her.
He leaves, and she obeys.
Days pass. The beast wins his victory
and the sky flashes red.
In excitement, knowing what this means,
without even feeling it,
her foot twitches, barely at all.
That very second the girl turns to stone.
The girl as well as the beast, far away,
and all the land between them.

The tree she sits on,
and the grass where her feet rest,
every blade.
The trees and the fruit that hangs from them,
fruit that was ripe and ready to be taken,
which she had resisted despite the heat
and the thirst and the days of waiting,
all now irreversibly set in place,
sucked of colour, never to feed insect,
bird or passer-by.
She had failed in so inconceivably small a way.
She had failed utterly.

Somatic anxiety
When I left behind the pursuit of gymnastics,
I remember that I missed only the chalking of hands
before mounting the bar or horse.

I think it was more
than simply missing the feeling of the powder,
softer than talc, and the creak of your hand
pushing down into the barrel.
More likely it was the fact that the chalk
was being relied upon for grip.
When something is being relied upon
it can feasibly malfunction
and any failure cannot be said to be your fault alone.

Trampolining is complete exposure:
just your body, the air around it,
rotation, momentum –
too much or not enough –
red cross, red cross, red cross,
air.

Competitive trait anxiety

When, as an adult,
I read Leanne Shapton's *Swimming Studies*,
an account of her years as a competitive swimmer,
I felt I understood her in a profound way.
Her words, 'I wasn't the best; I was relatively fast. I trained,
ate, travelled, and showered with the best in the country,
but wasn't the best; I was pretty good.'
could have been pulled straight out of my head.
I shared almost every feeling she recounted.
But, even now, with it all behind her,
her need to be in water seems compulsive.
It is her element.
Air was not mine.

Arousal

My hair was French plaited before each competition.
Neat, tight, no strays, set to solidity with hairspray.
The pull at the temples was a
grounding in the body, a fixing.

Stress

I have no memory of how I managed
my periods during competitions, when no clothing is allowed
besides the leotard in its infallible and total purity.
Very quickly after my periods began
I developed an irrational – or arguably absolutely rational –
fear of inserting tampons and can't recall
that I ever used one for the purposes of competing.

One afternoon, probably in the late 1990s,
I saw an open newspaper on the kitchen counter.
The newspaper reported on the intensive regime
of a famous Russian gymnast which, retrospectively,

seemed to imply a level of cruelty had been exercised
which we would never allow at home.
A result of this regime was that the gymnast –
pictured in pose on the beam, arms extended behind her head,
rib cage protruding, lower back very curved –
had ceased to have periods.
She had been pushed too far.

VI *Teeth*

At a point, many years ago,
dreams about my teeth became so constant and graphic
that I was able to talk to myself within my dream,
making assurances that, though my teeth might be loosening and falling,
or growing rapidly from both rows to such a length
that I resembled a mutant rat before they snapped into pieces,
I was very much in my bed asleep, all my teeth quiet in my head.

. . .

During the 2012 London Olympics
I watched my former synchronised trampolining partner
compete for Great Britain.

I watched her on my laptop,
with my mouth slightly open,
wondering how did she do it, how did she push through.

. . .

If you had an accident
when performing a certain move, you had to do that move again immediately,
before the fear set in.
Jump back on the horse.

64

. . .

In my dreams, when I am trying to escape danger
I move down the street in huge somersaults,
over fences, over water. I never run.

. . .

A leotard is like a second skin.
Black and green lycra,
red, white and navy velvet,
bright pink velvet.
Wriggled into and peeled off.

. . .

The lights in hotel rooms:
red dot on TV; blue dot on TV;
slice coming from under the bathroom door, pushed to;
sliver between the curtains;
digital alarm clock, blinking;
line underneath the room's door, from the hall,
which leads to the fire exit at one end,
memorised in the event of smoke from fire.
A constellation around mum, dad, brother, sleeping.
A map to memorise in the event of waking,
needing reassurance that you are not dead.

VII *Animal on a string*

As I got older my bodily fears –
my fears about what I couldn't control
with regard to my body,

my perception of my brain as the saboteur
at the helm of my body –
became more severe.
I added to the fear of throwing myself
in the wrong direction
or leaping off the trampoline sideways,
a fear of my neck snapping backwards,
a fear of my teeth snapping closed and biting off my tongue,
of the tendons in my legs snapping.
What did my body contain that couldn't snap?

The main hall I trained in was set up
with either four or six trampolines in a grid,
with no spaces between them.
I often fantasised that I would halt
at the very highest point in a jump
and hover there, then begin to circle
the perimeter of the sports hall
looking down on the array of beds with their red crosses
and select which one to descend to, very slowly.

Friends used to ask me if trampolining felt like flying
to which I replied that it did
knowing it was the answer they wanted.

When I sit alone in my garden,
I track the journeys of individual bees.
Snapdragon – dahlia – verbena – salvia –
dandelion – sedum – broad bean flowers –
cosmos – cosmos – cosmos –
willing them to settle.

VIII *Hymenoptera is the order of insects that includes ants, wasps and bees, from the Greek hymen (membrane) plus pteron (wing)*

At breakfast I sat down at a table beside a low brick wall
upon which had been placed a small white plate.

The inner circle of the plate was dotted with pieces of sausage,
red and chopped into small chunks.

Beyond the plate was a bed of rosemary, then olive trees,
flits of small brown birds, then the flat expanse of the Aegean sea.

The purpose of the plate was to act as a distraction for the wasps,
who otherwise bothered the guests throughout their morning meal.

The bait was working – the plate playing host to between five and ten
wasps at any given moment. The plate was a source of constant movement

in my peripheral vision, the bodies of the wasps catching the light,
treading over the meat, occasionally taking flight to hover and land again.

The amount of sausage diminished
through the course of breakfast as the wasps filled with meat.

IX *Lake Garda, Italy*

At the age of twenty-seven
I got on a trampoline again.
A group of us sat in a café by the side of the lake,
drinking beer. Me and the older son
from the yellow hospital room decided to bounce.
He had continued to train and compete
into his early twenties and even on a small,

meshed trampoline designed for children,
he was stunning.
I was in the early stages of drunkenness
and wearing a long black sundress.
I limited myself to the handful of moves –
mostly simple somersaults – that I'd done so many
thousands of times I didn't even need to think.
A group of children gathered to watch us.

I did one move, a lazy back –
a straight backwards somersault landing in a front drop –
many times. The motion of it
is very pleasing and mimics the way a cherub
might come to rest on a cloud.
I was warned many times, before puberty came,
that once my breasts grew
it would start to hurt to land on my front.
It never did.

Afterwards we sat back down,
slightly out of breath. My little cousin came over
and stood beside me, told me to stay very still.
I did as instructed, tilted my head back
and he placed a small plastic bug on my nose.
I focused on the toy's many bent legs,
its black, painted eyes. It balanced there.
My cousin was delighted.
He removed the bug.

In *Swimming Studies*, Shapton says,
'When I swim now I step into the water as though
absentmindedly touching a scar.'
The mesh had felt warm and safe on my bare feet.
Being upside down, in the air, was completely usual.

Nothing was ripped apart.

My feet tingled with the memory of it.

It felt like old knowledge.

CPSIA information can be obtained
at www.ICGtesting.com
Printed in the USA
JSHW041738050821
17601JS00002B/2